PAPIER-MÂCHÉ

Gareth Stevens Publishing
A WORLD ALMANAC EDUCATION GROUP COMPANY

Please visit our web site at: www.garethstevens.com
For a free color catalog describing Gareth Stevens Publishing's
list of high-quality books and multimedia programs,
call 1-800-542-2595 (USA) or 1-800-387-3178 (Canada).
Gareth Stevens Publishing's fax: (414) 332-3567.

Library of Congress Cataloging-in-Publication Data

Papier-mâché.
        p. cm. — (Let's create!)
        Includes bibliographical references.
        Summary: Provides step-by-step instructions for making crafts
using papier-mâché, plastic or clay molds, crumpled newspaper,
and various finishes.
        ISBN 0-8368-4017-8 (lib. bdg.)
        1. Papier-mâché—Juvenile literature. [1. Papier-mâché.
2. Handicraft.] I. Title. II. Series.
TT871.P35313   2004
745.54'2—dc22   2003057360

This North American edition first published in 2004 by
Gareth Stevens Publishing
A World Almanac Education Group Company
330 West Olive Street, Suite 100
Milwaukee, WI 53212 USA

First published as *¡Vamos a crear! Papel maché* with an original copyright © 2002
by Parramón Ediciones, S.A., – World Rights, text and illustrations by Parramón's
Editorial Team. This U.S. edition copyright © 2004 by Gareth Stevens, Inc.
Additional end matter copyright © 2004 by Gareth Stevens, Inc.

English Translation: Colleen Coffey
Gareth Stevens Series Editor: Dorothy L. Gibbs
Gareth Stevens Designer: Katherine A. Goedheer

Printed in Spain

1 2 3 4 5 6 7 8 9 08 07 06 05 04

Table of Contents

Introduction

Papier-mâché is nothing more than torn paper mixed with glue. *Mâché* comes from the French word "mâcher" (mah-shay), which means to tear apart or to chew. *Mâchoire* (mosh-wahr) is a French word for "jaw." In the English language, papier-mâché refers to torn, glued paper that is molded into shapes.

You can make papier-mâché from almost any type of paper, including newspaper, magazine pages, construction paper, and tissue paper. For recycling reasons, however, newspaper is the type most commonly used. Thin cardboard can be used, too. A kind of thick, soft art paper, called gray bogus paper (pictured at the top of page 5), looks and feels like very thin cardboard and works very well for papier-mâché projects. You can also buy instant papier-mâché mix, which is a paper powder you mix with water. The instant mixture is very easy to model.

This book shows you different ways to work with papier-mâché, using clay molds, plastic molds, cardboard tubes, egg cartons, balloons, and many other materials. Its twelve colorful projects also show you how to apply different finishes, including paint, construction paper, tissue paper, and even aluminum foil. Designer Dishware turns a plain plastic bowl into an *objet d'art*. Funny Face is a clown mask that begins with a balloon. Box Turtle is actually an egg carton. And whoever thought that a cardboard toilet paper tube could be a rocket to the Moon?

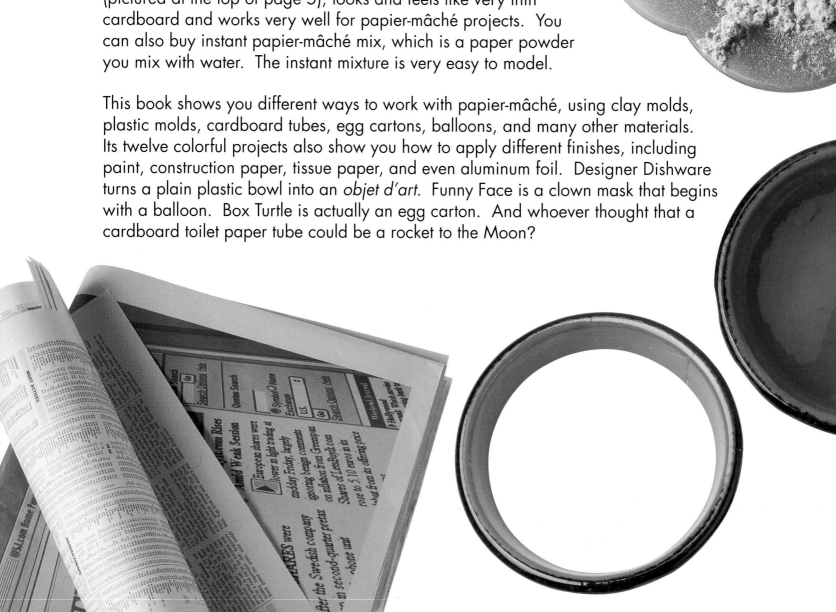

Most of the tools you will need to make these projects are things you use every day, either at school or at home. They include scissors, glue, paints, clay, tape, string, pieces of wire, and, of course, just about any kind of paper.

The projects in this book use water-soluable powdered glue or white glue diluted with water to make the papier-mâché. Either type of glue can be used for any of the projects.

Some projects tell you to soak the paper in water, while others do not. Wet paper is not always necessary, but, for certain projects, wet paper is easier to shape and gives your finished piece more detail.

Several projects also tell you to cover the dried papier-mâché figure with plaster paste. To make the paste, use plaster of paris, which is a chalky white powder. You may have used plaster of paris for other kinds of art or craft projects. Mix plaster of paris powder with water until it is about as thick as paint. Remember that plaster paste hardens quickly, especially if it is too thick.

Watch for special instructions at the end of each project to try other great ideas. Sometimes, making just one small change creates a very different result.

Papier-mâché is so easy to do. All you need is some paper and glue!

Friendly Ghost

Most people just use a white sheet to make a ghost. You can be more creative! Use sheets of gray paper and paint your ghost a bright color.

1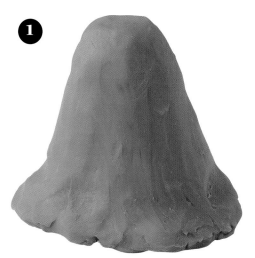

1 With a big lump of any color modeling clay, form the shape of a bell.

2

2 Mix powdered glue with water, then tear sheets of gray art paper into small pieces. Soak the pieces of paper in the glue. Cover the clay figure with the glue-soaked paper.

You will need:
- modeling clay
- powdered glue
- gray art paper
- scissors
- paintbrushes
- plaster of paris
- blue, black, and white paints

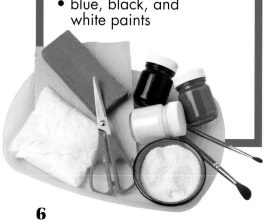

3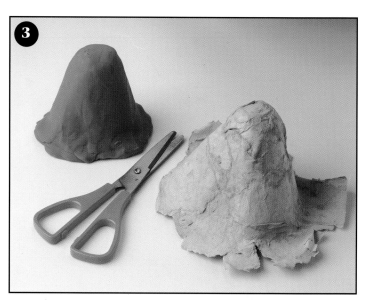

3 When the paper is dry, remove the clay. Use scissors to cut around the bottom of the paper figure to even out the edge.

4 Brush on a coat of plaster paste (see page 5). When the figure is completely dry, paint it blue.

This little ghost is a breeze to make — and it will not scare your friends away!

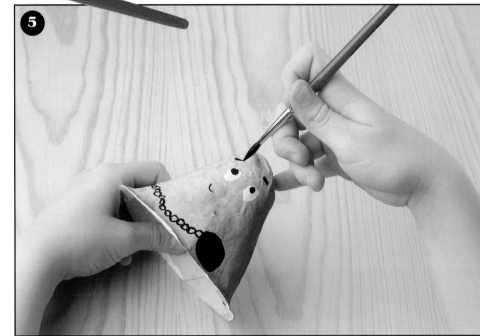

5 When the blue paint is dry, use black and white paints to add eyes, eyebrows, a mouth, and a ball and chain.

Another Great Idea!
Make lots of ghosts! If you paint them all different colors and give them all different expressions, you will have a ghostly family.

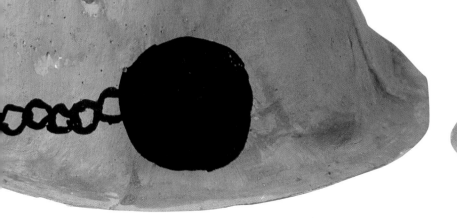

Long-Legged Bird

When you make this exotic bird, be sure to give it brightly colored tissue-paper feathers — the brighter, the better!

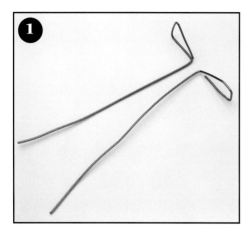

1 Cut two pieces of wire. Make each piece 6 inches (15 centimeters) long. Bend one end of each piece of wire into the shape of a triangle. The triangles will form the bird's feet.

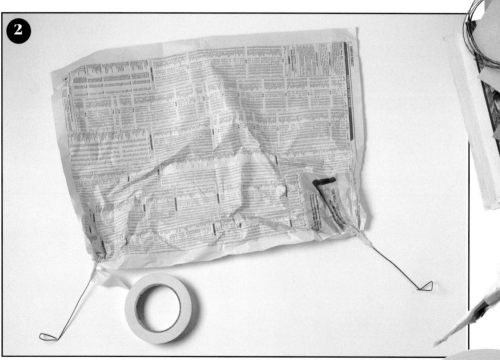

2 Use masking tape to attach the straight end of each piece of wire to the two lower corners of a page of newspaper.

3 Crumple the newspaper to shape the body and the head of the bird, then wrap masking tape around the newspaper to hold the shape.

4 Mix powdered glue with water. Soak torn pieces of gray art paper in the glue. Cover the body, head, beak, and wire feet with glue-soaked paper. Cut shapes out of gray paper that look like wings and a tail and attach them to the bird's body.

5 When the gray paper is completely dry, brush glue all over it and attach torn pieces of green, orange, and yellow tissue paper.

6 To make the bird's eyes, roll small pieces of orange, red, and white modeling clay into little balls. Stack the balls one on top of the other — first orange, then red, then white. Using your fingers, press each eye onto the bird's head.

Let your imagination decide what shape your bird will be. Then, imagine other animals and make them, too!

Another Great Idea!
Glue the feet to a cardboard or wooden platform so your bird can stand by itself.

Hot-Air Balloon

Would you like to float along with the clouds? Use a party balloon to make this papier-mâché balloon and let your imagination soar.

You will need:
- balloon
- powdered glue
- fuschia, green, and purple colored paper
- paintbrushes
- clay pick
- red string
- gray art paper
- glass
- orange and red paints
- scissors
- clear tape

1 Blow up a balloon and knot it to hold in the air. Mix powdered glue with water, then tear colored paper into strips. Coat the paper strips with glue and cover the balloon with them, leaving some space uncovered at the bottom.

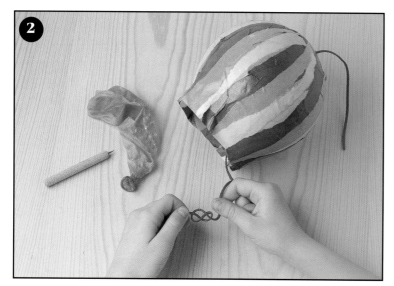

2 When the paper is dry, use a clay pick to pop the balloon and to make a hole at the top of the paper balloon. Thread a loop of red string through the hole and knot the ends inside the balloon.

3 Tear gray art paper into strips and soak the strips in glue. Press the glue-soaked strips into a glass so they cover the inside of the glass.

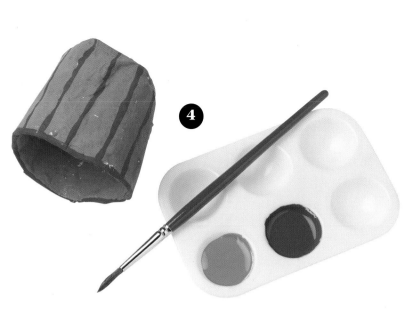

4 When the gray paper is dry, take it out of the glass. This shape is the balloon's basket. Paint the basket orange with red stripes.

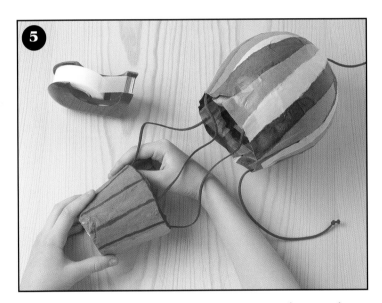

5 Cut four pieces of red string. Make each piece 8 inches (20 cm) long. Tape one end of each piece of string to the balloon and the other end to the basket, leaving approximately the same amount of space between strings.

Another Great Idea!
Cover the basket of your hot-air balloon with string or yarn and add other details, such as sandbags made of tissue paper, hanging from pieces of string.

Hang your balloon from the ceiling and prepare for an adventure. Think of the places you could go in this unusual form of transportation.

Handsome Hanger

Your pretty clothes deserve good-looking hangers. Decorating hangers is easy — and a lot of fun. Why not try it yourself?

1 Mix powdered glue with water. Cover a wooden coat hanger with several layers of newspaper strips that have been brushed with glue.

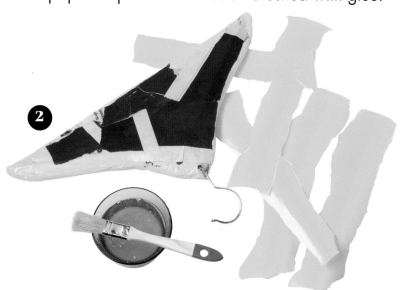

2 Cover the newspaper with glue-coated strips of yellow wrapping paper.

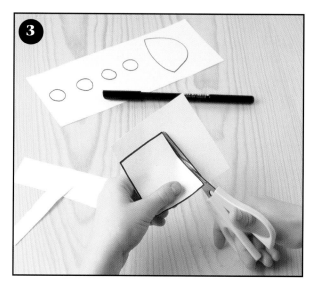

3 On a piece of white paper, draw a pocket, a neck piece, and four buttons, then cut out the drawings.

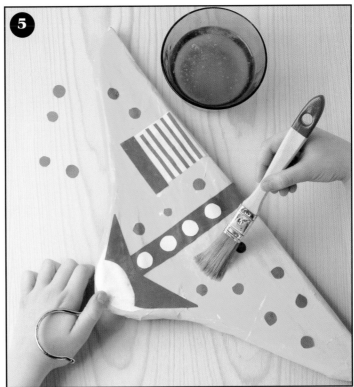

4 On a sheet of purple paper, draw a collar, a long strip for the buttons, some stripes for the pocket, and a lot of polka dots. Cut out all the drawings.

5 Glue the white and purple pieces onto the yellow wrapping paper to make one side of the hanger look like a shirt. Brush a coat of glue over the decorated surface.

A decorated hanger can add color to your closet and give your wardrobe more pizzazz!

Another Great Idea!
Add a decorative paper tie or a paper bow to dress up your "shirt" hanger.

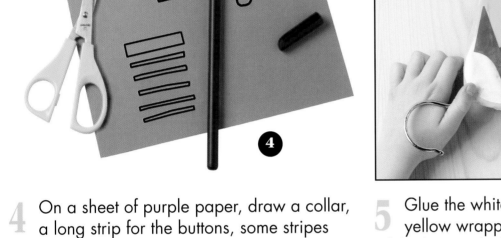

Little Red Devil

From head to trident, this bright red hand puppet is devilishly delightful and sinfully easy to make.

You will need:

- newspaper
- masking tape
- orange cardboard
- white glue
- paintbrushes
- instant papier-mâché
- plaster of paris
- red, white, and black paints
- red felt
- marker
- scissors
- needle
- black thread
- glue stick
- aluminum foil
- liquid school glue

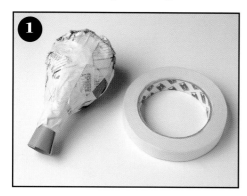

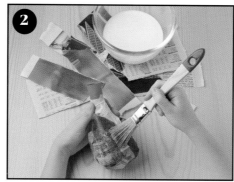

1 Crumple newspaper into a ball and hold it together with masking tape. Roll a small piece of orange cardboard into a tube that fits over your middle finger and tape the tube closed. Tape the ball and the tube together.

2 Dilute white glue with water. Wrap strips of newspaper around the newspaper ball and the cardboard tube, brushing each strip with the diluted glue. This step forms the head and neck of the puppet.

3 Use instant papier-mâché to shape horns and a nose on the puppet's head and brush plaster paste (see page 5) over the entire head.

4 When the head is completely dry, paint it red, then use white and black paints to make eyes and a mouth.

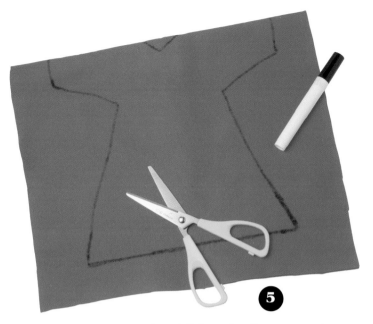

5 Fold a piece of red felt in half. Draw the shape of a dress on the felt so the tops of the arms are along the fold. Cut out the dress and cut a V-shaped opening at the center of the fold.

6 Use a needle and black thread to sew the sides of the dress and under the arms. Do not sew across the bottom of the dress. Leave the neck and armholes open, too.

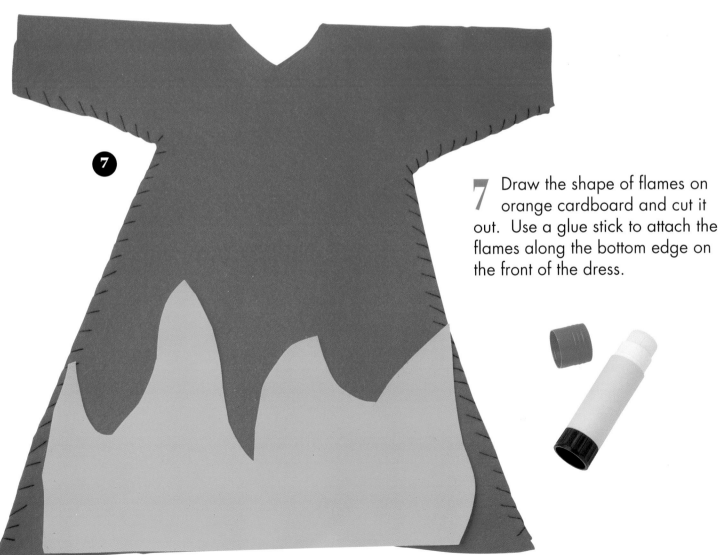

7 Draw the shape of flames on orange cardboard and cut it out. Use a glue stick to attach the flames along the bottom edge on the front of the dress.

8 Shape instant papier-mâché around your index finger to make the puppet's two hands.

9 When the hands are dry, paint them red.

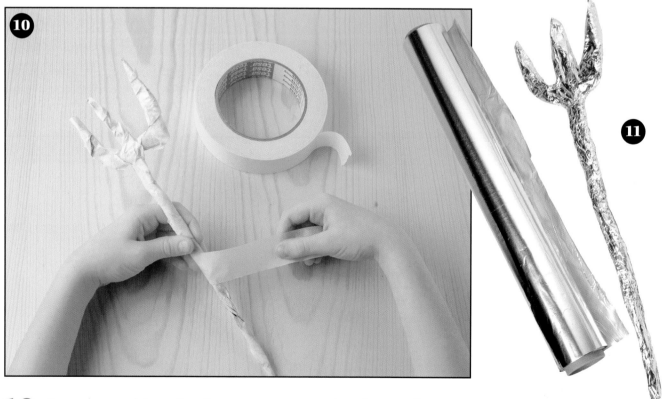

10 Form long, thin rolls of newspaper into the shape of a trident. Wrap masking tape around the newspaper to hold the shape.

11 Cover the trident with aluminum foil.

12 To make a holder for the trident, cut two parallel slits into the front of the dress, above the flames. Slide the handle of the trident into the top slit and out through the bottom slit. Finish the puppet by attaching its head and its hands to the red felt dress with liquid school glue.

Now all you have to do is create a story. Your little red devil is ready to play the leading role.

Another Great Idea!
Design a different dress, using materials such as plastic and crepe paper, to create a very different puppet character.

Designer Dishware

Use a plastic bowl as a mold to make a fancy papier-mâché bowl. Decorate your bowl any way you like. You're the designer!

1 Dilute white glue with water, then tear newspaper into wide strips. Line the inside of a plastic bowl with newspaper strips, one layer at a time, brushing the diluted glue over each layer. Use your fingers to press the glued strips against the sides of the bowl.

2 Fold any newspaper that is sticking out toward the inside of the bowl.

You will need:
- white glue
- newspaper
- plastic bowl
- paintbrushes
- instant papier-mâché
- plaster of paris
- orange, blue, and white paints

3 When the paper bowl is completely dry, take it out of the plastic bowl. Use instant papier-mâché to make a thick rim around the edge of the bowl.

18

4 Brush plaster paste (see page 5) over the entire bowl. After the paste dries, paint the bowl orange with a blue-and-white striped rim.

5 With the tip of your finger, paint blue and white polka dots all the way around the outside of the bowl.

Use this decorative bowl to store colored pencils, coins, or any other small items, but it should never be used for food or beverages.

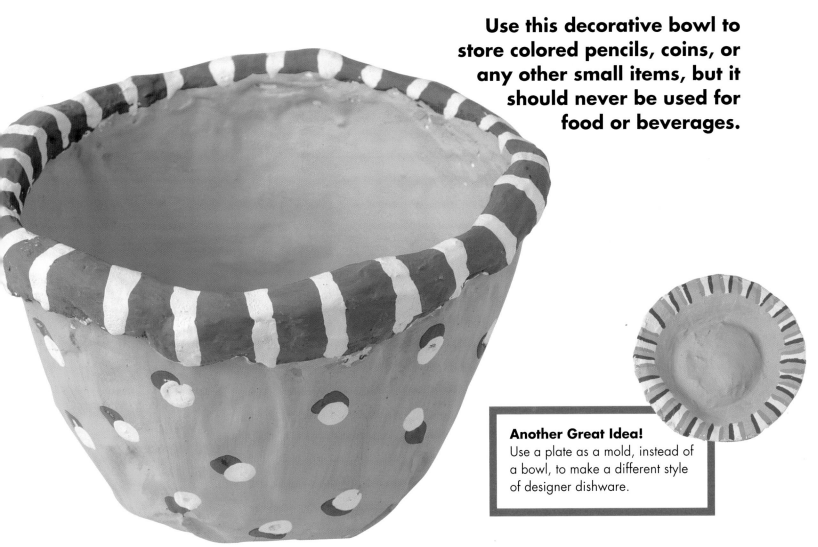

Another Great Idea!
Use a plate as a mold, instead of a bowl, to make a different style of designer dishware.

Moon Rocket

With a little imagination, even a papier-mâché rocket can take you to the Moon. Follow these five easy steps, and you'll be on your way.

You will need:
- white glue
- gray art paper
- newspaper
- 2 cardboard toilet paper tubes
- scissors
- black, white, red, and orange paints
- paintbrushes
- round toothpick
- plaster of paris

1 Dilute white glue with water, then tear gray art paper into strips. Form the shape of a rocket by using glue-soaked paper strips to attach a ball of newspaper to one end of a cardboard toilet paper tube.

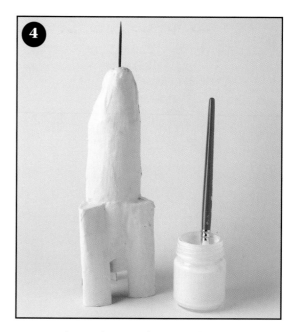

2 Cut another toilet paper tube, lengthwise, into three equal pieces.

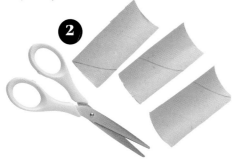

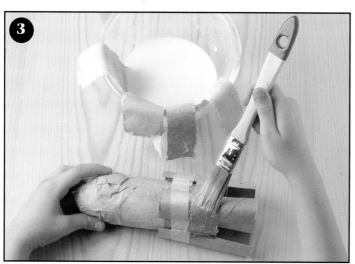

3 Using more glue-soaked strips of gray art paper, attach the three pieces of cardboard tube around the open end of the rocket to make booster engines.

4 When the rocket and boosters are dry, paint a round toothpick black and stick it into the tip of the rocket. Cover the entire rocket with plaster paste (see page 5) and paint it white.

5 To decorate the rocket, paint red squares around the body and paint the tip of the rocket black. Paint the tops of the booster engines red and paint the bottoms orange, making the orange paint look like flames.

10, 9, 8, 7, 6, 5, 4, 3, 2, 1. . .
BLAST OFF!

Another Great Idea!
Use modeling clay or instant paper-mâché to make the rocket's booster engines.

Box Turtle

Making this friendly turtle is fun — and fast! Its shell is a cardboard egg carton.

1 Mix powdered glue with water. Cut out four rounded feet and a triangle-shaped tail from a large piece of gray art paper. Glue the paper shapes to the top of an open cardboard egg carton so that two feet are sticking out on each long side of the carton and the tail is sticking out at one short end.

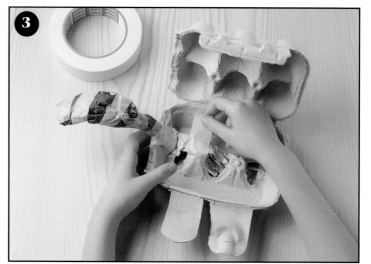

3 Attach the neck to the egg carton on the end across from the tail. Cover the head and neck with glued-soaked strips of newspaper and glue the egg carton closed with more glued strips of newspaper.

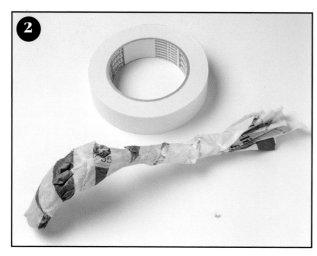

2 Crumple newspaper and wrap it with masking tape to shape the turtle's head and neck.

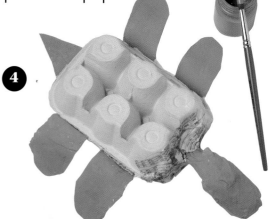

4 When all of the newspaper is dry, paint the head, feet, and tail of the turtle green.

22

5 Paint the shell of the turtle orange, with green and yellow details. Paint a white circle with a black center on each side of the head for eyes and paint yellow claws on each foot. To finish, paint an orange mouth and a black nose, then paint yellow stripes across the tail.

Your colorful, painted turtle may be too slow to win a race, but it's sure to win smiles.

Another Great Idea!
Keep the egg carton open, instead of gluing it closed. Then you will be able to keep small treasures, or anything else you want, inside your turtle.

Tipsy Tumbler

Imagine a roly-poly doll that never falls down. Then, make one!

1 Line half of a plastic sphere with modeling clay, pressing the clay against the inside of the sphere with your fingers.

2 Place the other half of the plastic sphere on top of the clay-lined half. Wrap masking tape around the sphere to hold the halves together.

3 Mix powdered glue with water. Cover the sphere with glued strips of gray art paper.

4 When the glued paper is dry, paint the top half of the sphere pink and the bottom, clay-lined half blue.

24

5 Paint hair and a face on the pink top of the sphere and paint decorative stripes on the blue bottom.

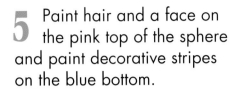

6 To make a hat, cut one cup out of a cardboard egg carton. Paint the outside of the cup blue. When the blue paint is dry, decorate the cup with white and green painted polka dots. Glue the hat to the top of your roly-poly tipsy tumbler.

❻

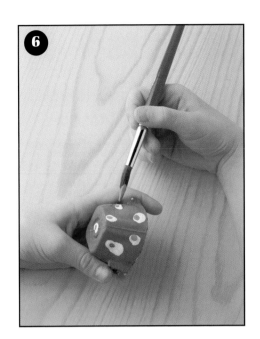

Push the tipsy tumbler forward and backward and all around. It will always tip over but never falls down!

Another Great Idea!
If you don't have a plastic sphere, use modeling clay to shape the bottom of the doll and make the top out of crumpled newspaper. Then cover the whole figure with glued paper.

25

Funny Face

You'll have to use your head to make this clever clown mask, but don't use it to shape the mask's papier-mâché face. Use a balloon instead.

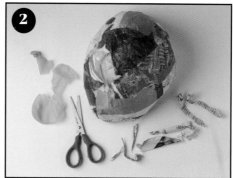

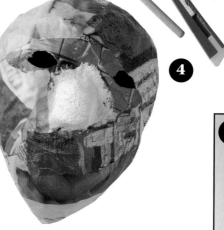

1 Dilute white glue with water. Blow up a balloon and knot the end to hold in the air. Cover one side of the balloon, halfway around, with damp strips of newspaper, brushing each strip of news-paper with diluted white glue as you place it on the balloon.

2 When the newspaper is dry, pop the balloon and cut off the uneven ends of the newspaper strips to shape the edge of the mask.

3 To make a nose for the mask, roll instant papier-mâché into a ball and press it onto the center of the mask.

4 Ask an adult to cut eye-holes in the mask with a razor knife and to make small breathing holes below the nose with a clay pick. Also use the clay pick to make a hole near the edge on each side of the mask, just below the eyes.

5 Cover the entire mask with plaster paste (see page 5). When the mask is completely dry, paint it any way you like.

6 To make the clown's hair, use a glue stick to attach a coiled strip of green garland on each side of the clown's head.

7 Thread black elastic string through the two holes in the edge of the mask. Knot both ends of the string to hold it in place.

When you want to make people laugh, put on your funny face. But don't be surprised if no one recognizes you!

Another Great Idea!
Use instant papier-mâché to shape ears, as well a nose, to make an animal mask. Attach ears, instead of hair, to the top of the mask — or add both ears and hair!

Mâchémobile

Trying to figure out how you made this awesome automobile will drive your friends crazy. The secret? Cardboard tubes and papier-mâché!

You will need:
- powdered glue
- paintbrushes
- 5 cardboard toilet paper tubes
- clothespins
- newspaper
- plaster of paris
- green, white, black, and yellow paints

1 Mix powdered glue with water. Glue together three cardboard tubes in a horizontal row. Glue two more tubes on top of them (as shown). Hold the tubes in place with a few clothespins until the glue dries.

2 Tear strips of newspaper. Brushing each strip with glue, wrap them around the stack of cardboard tubes until the tubes are completely covered with newspaper.

3 When the newspaper is dry, cover the entire car with plaster paste (see page 5) and paint it green.

28

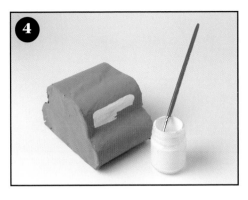

4 Paint the windows of the car and the front and back license plates white.

5 Paint wheels and other details on the car black and paint yellow lights on both the front and back ends.

This clever car is a great decoration, but it is also sturdy enough for playtime.

Another Great Idea!
Use more cardboard toilet paper tubes or use longer cardboard tubes from rolls of paper towels to make larger vehicles, such as tractors, trucks, or vans.

Easter Bonnet

A yellow flower adds a splash of color to this pretty purple hat. Wear it proudly at a party, in a parade, or for any other special occasion.

1 Cut strips of purple paper so they are a little longer than the diameter of the bowl you will be using.

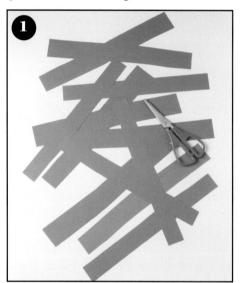

2 Mix powdered glue with water. Cover the bowl with a layer of purple strips, without using glue. Then, add one or two more layers of purple strips that have been brushed with glue.

You will need:
- scissors
- purple paper
- bowl
- powdered glue
- newspaper
- masking tape
- green and white paints
- paintbrushes
- yellow cardboard
- white glue

3 When the glue is completely dry, take the plate away and trim around the edge of the hat to make it round and even. Make small cuts into the edge of the brim, all the way around, to create fringe.

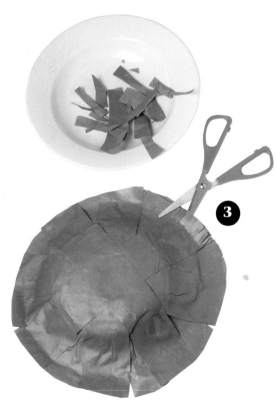

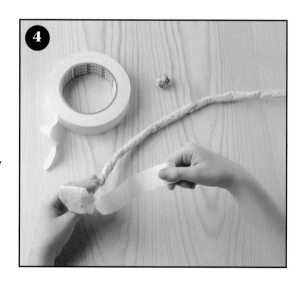

4 To make the stem for the flower decoration, roll newspaper into a thin, snakelike strand that is long enough to fit around the crown of the hat. Wrap masking tape around the newspaper and paint the entire stem green.

30

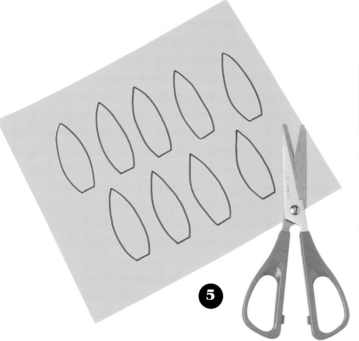

5 Draw nine flower petals on a piece of yellow cardboard and cut them out. Use white glue to attach the petals to the end of the green stem.

6 Push a small ball of newspaper into the center of the petals and paint it white. Use white glue to attach the flower stem to the top of the hat.

Just wait till you see how elegant you look in this fancy hat!

Another Great Idea!
Instead of adding a flower, glue a long piece of wide yellow ribbon around the top of the hat and let the ends of the ribbon hang as streamers from the back of the hat.

31

Glossary

coiled: rolled into a spiral shape

dependable: able to be counted on or relied upon; trustworthy

diameter: the distance across the center of a circle

dilute: make thinner or more fluid, usually by mixing with water or another liquid

exotic: unusual, as if from a different part of the world

flexible: able to be bent

fuschia: a deep, bright pink color named for the blossom of the fuschia plant

garland: a long, ropelike decoration made of fringed paper

horizontal: level; straight across

model: (v) to form or shape

objet d'art: an artistic item or object

pizzazz: liveliness; excitement; glamour

sphere: a ball- or globe-shaped object

trident: a broom-sized instrument with one end shaped like a three-pronged fork

water-soluable: able to be dissolved in water

More Books to Read

Crafts from Papier-Mâché. Step by Step (series). Violaine Lamerand (Bridgestone Books)

Creating with Papier-Mâché. Crafts for All Seasons (series). Victoria Seix (Blackbirch Press)

Papier-Mâché. Kids Can Do It (series). Renee Schwarz (Econoclad Books)

Papier-Mâché. Let's Start! (series). Wayne South (Silver Dolphin)

Play with Papier-Mâché. Play with Crafts (series). Susan Moxley (Carolrhoda Books)

Web Sites

Family Fun Activities & Crafts: Best Papier-Mache Recipe. family.go.com/crafts/buildmodel/expert/dony0300aapapier/

EnchantedLearning.com's Papier-Mâché Crafts. www.enchantedlearning.com/crafts/papiermache/